Random Commuter Observations

Living the Dream on the Way to Work

Michael Lewis

A POST HILL PRESS BOOK

ISBN: 978-1-68261-641-3
ISBN (eBook): 978-1-68261-642-0

Random Commuter Observations
Living the Dream on the Way to Work
© 2018 by Michael Lewis

Cover art by Cody Corcoran

Post Hill Press, LLC
New York • Nashville
posthillpress.com

Published in the United States of America

This book is dedicated to all the poor slobs who have to endure the sights, smells, and sounds of a commute from Hell...or rather, *through* Hell.

And to my buddy John Hetlyn, who's been enduring like a champ an hours-long commute from Orange County, New York, to Midtown, New York, for more than thirty years.

ACKNOWLEDGMENTS

I want to thank my family
—Amy, Sam, and Syd—
for putting up with me every day, as I dragged
my cranky commuter self back and forth.

Thanks to Steve Spignesi, author/coauthor extraordinaire, great friend, confidante, sounding board.

Much love/hugs/thanks to superagent Marilyn Allen.

My appreciation to Anthony Ziccardi, Michael Wilson, Billie Brownell, and the rest of the gang at Post Hill Press.

I want to acknowledge all my friends who commute every day, via train, bus, auto, other(?). Special shout out to those who shared their own Random Commuter Observations with me: Chris Anderson, Eric Brandon, Gail Burke, Bob Jenny, Rachel Montgomery, Joe Potestivo, Janice Robertson, and Steven Schragis. Hope I didn't forget anyone.

Finally, thank you to all the bosses I've worked for over the years. Only one of them ever "let me go" against my wishes, from a job that forced me to commute to NYC for ninety minutes each way (if everything ran on time) and keep a journal of my experiences. And that's how this book was born. So at least something good came out of that job!

CONTENTS

CONTENTS

INTRODUCTION

If I were a nobler man, I would say I'm thinking about my fellow commuter as I write these words, but alas, I'm not. Any of us who commute know that it's a selfish endeavor. All you want to do is get away from these herds of people, as fast as possible, to get to a job you may not be thrilled with but, hey, it pays the bills. All you're thinking about is yourself—or, at the end of the day, what (hopefully) better things await you when you get home. As Rodney Dangerfield once quipped, "Look out for number one. Just don't step in number two."

Among the working class for more than forty years, I'm trying to think back to the first time I ever commuted to work. I can't remember the specifics, but I do know I rode my bike to work back then—to a little ice cream place on the other side of town. My commuting evolved as my career evolved—from driving (enduring one job that took over ninety minutes to reach, without traffic), and finally to mass transit. My last commute was to New York City for 18 months, and consisted of two trains, sandwiched between a few blocks' walk on either end. The commute wasn't horrible, I guess, as many have endured tougher treks. But like any commute, it does wear on you. You have no other options than to be engulfed in a sea of humanity, all rushing alongside you. Excruciating crowds, cancelled trains, derailings, track repairs, train crashes…looking back, I realize how precarious it was on a daily basis, how only one minor thing could cause frustrating delays, frayed nerves, and aggravation as I *just wanted to get home*! I think commuting's going to get worse before it can get better, but hopefully, someday, this country can finally invest in its infrastructure and make life a little bit easier for working folk.

To while away the hours along the way, day-to-day, I played Sudoku, read the paper, listened to music, and people-watched. You can learn a lot about humanity, and where we're headed, by people-watching. I took notes about what I observed, sharing them to Facebook on occasion. My snarky observations seemed to strike a chord with people, so I decided to collect everything into a book—the book you've got in your hands at this moment! Enjoy.

RCO: In NYC, no matter where you stand, or where you walk, you're always in someone's way. And someone's always in yours.

RCO: Watch the gap between the train and the platform. Let me rephrase that: Try not to slip into the gap between the train and the platform, because the platform is covered in ice.

RCO: The other day—within five minutes of each other—two people started to sit down next to me, looked at me, then walked to another seat.

RCO: Saying "excuse me" doesn't make it okay to barrel into everyone on a crowded train. Instead, how about waiting for the next train?

RCO: I'll give a dollar to every Salvation Army person I walk past who's standing there and ringing that bell. If you're not making the effort to ring the bell—or, worse yet, you've got a boom box there blasting hip hop—color me gone.

RCO: Let me see if I've got this straight: You're going to inconvenience thousands of regular commuters, people just trying to get home from a long day's work, asking them to find a new track, for the sake of a few hundred drunken slobs on their way to a football game?

RCO: Today marks the first day I ever saw a live rat running around on the street, in rush hour, broad daylight. About the size of a small chihuahua.

RCO: Commuting every day, at the same times, you start seeing some of the same people. You're often "train friends" with some of them, although you don't even know their names. So I'd like to take some time to introduce you to my commuting friends: Hey, there's Chewbacca. He likes to bite his nails and cuticles like a squirrel nibbling an ear of corn. Never mind that his hands are dirty having touched every handrail and door handle from his office to here.

RCO: I guess from the perspective of the people who run into me every day as I commute, I'm running into them.

RCO: NYC pedestrians are rude year-round, but in winter their excuse for running into you is that they're in a rush to get out of the cold.

COMMUTERS WARY

RCO: Hey, Port Authority bus terminal has free Wi-Fi. Maybe this crappy commuting situation won't be so bad after all.

RCO: The guy who sat next to me the other day smelled so bad that when I took a nap, I dreamed I was in a locker room.

(Credit: Public domain)

RCO: Not gonna lie—as the train approaches the station, and I get closer to the yellow line, I always take a quick look around to make sure there are no psychotic people about who could potentially push me onto the tracks.

RCO: I miss my regular commute, on my usual dirty, sweaty train.

RCO: I'd rather walk behind someone with horrendous body odor than follow along behind someone who's smoking as they walk.

RCO: Personal space is nonexistent. So is dignity.

RCO: Alternate merge rules don't apply when 1,000 inconsiderate commuters jockey their way from the platform to the stairs.

RCO: Gee, thanks, Pokémon Go—like people need more things to distract them as they're walking along and not paying attention.

RCO: School's out, which means there will now be twice as many aimless people on the sidewalk.

RCO: Strangely, at least 38 percent of the time I get a coffee, the "spout" on the plastic lid is lined up with the crease on the cup. (I always move it.)

RCO: I'm only going to hold the door open for you for so long.

RCO: More people are wearing brown shoes today than any other color.

RCO: The temperature in a naturally occurring cave averages around 49–52 degrees. The average temperature year-round in Penn Station is 87–93 degrees. And smells worse.

RCO: Riding in a crowded train is like Hot Yoga without the movement.

RCO: Most people walk too slowly for my liking.

RCO: Those of you who are met at your train station by your spouse and young kids, who joyfully run to greet you—cherish those fleeting moments. They're not going to be there to greet you every day. They might not even notice you were gone.

RCO: An unforeseen negative consequence of disallowing smoking in buildings in NYC is that now every smoker stands on the sidewalk, or walks in front of me as I walk down the sidewalk.

RCO: Standing up, getting ready to leave a crowded train, and collecting all your things is like Superman getting changed in a phone booth.

RCO: OMG, a new train schedule waiting for me on my seat! It's like Christmas morning!

RCO: Ghost town in Secaucus Junction this morning but madhouse in Penn Station. Goes to show you never can tell.

COMMUTERS FACED WITH OPTIONS, NONE OF THEM GREAT

RCO: Just as water seeks a level, the jerks who run onto the train right as the doors are closing seek to fill any available space they find. If you're on the train ahead of them, stake a claim to your spot and hold onto it for dear life, anticipating their arrival. Don't show any fear, or any daylight.

RCO: Just keep repeating to yourself that everything in this world is finite, as you endure another ridiculously overcrowded transfer train ride during which your every sense is assaulted.

RCO: Getting on at the transfer station is kinda like a carnival game. If you are standing on the platform as the train home arrives, at the exact spot where the doors will open, and you walk quicker than other entering passengers, you might have a shot at grabbing one of about six seats still available. If all of the above doesn't happen, you're standing.

RCO: Worse than a clueless cellphone gawker swerving aimlessly around a crowded sidewalk is a clueless traveler dragging fishtailing wheelie luggage around behind them.

RCO: That cigarette you inhaled shortly before sitting next to me on the train clings to you like a lovely French perfume. Not.

RCO: If you've got tuberculosis, stay home.

RCO: Sometimes I channel my inner O. J., running down the sidewalk to catch a train. Only without that whole murderous rampage and bloody glove thing.

RCO: More people go to work on Mondays than on Fridays.

RCO: Know what day it is. On St. Paddy's Day, your train may be filled with drunken, queasy revelers, so be alert and aware of your surroundings. (Thanks, Janice Robertson.)

RCO: To experience a less-crowded commute, work a 12-hour day. Turn the office lights on when you're the first one there in the morning, and turn them off at night when you're the last one to leave.

RCO: Wearing a backpack buys you a little extra personal space. So does claiming that you have sciatica.

RCO: Some people should have to pay for two train tickets.

RCO: An escalator that's off ain't nothin' but a staircase.

(Credit: Wikimedia Commons—This file is
licensed under the Creative Commons Attribution-
Share Alike 3.0 Unported license.)

TROUBLE ON THE TRACKS

RCO: Unless you're giving birth or on the way to putting out a fire, you don't deserve to get on or off the train any quicker than anyone else.

RCO: Legionnaires' Disease was invented on a NJ Transit train car.

RCO: The more uncomfortable and sardine-like your train ride is in the morning, the slower the train travels to Penn Station.

RCO: This dude smells like curry.

CONDEMNED TO PENN STATION HELL

RCO: Is the infrastructure crumbling faster than anyone's ability to repair and maintain it?

RCO: One of life's greatest disappointments—buying a dirty water dog and discovering after the first bite that it has no flavor, as it's been sitting in that water for a week. (Its gray color should have given it away.)

RCO: Maybe if we ignore problems with mass transit, they'll just go away.

RCO: Okay, what the hell just dripped on my head?!

RCO: Listen for the hiss of the air brakes releasing. That will (almost) prepare you for the violent whiplash movement as the train starts to leave the station.

RCO: The Quiet Car should be the same in every language.

RCO: Running down the sidewalk at rush hour to get to a train is like driving in a blizzard with your high beams on, and trying to avoid the snow hitting your windshield.

RCO: Never fails—the faster I try to get through Penn, the better chance I have of getting stuck behind a drunken sailor.

RCO: I'm convinced that surfers would make great commuters.

Meet my commuting friends:
There's Mr. Noodle. Like
the character from Sesame
Street, this clueless simpleton
is always unaware that he is
doing something wrong. Like
when everyone's standing on
the train platform while he
arrives late and then just runs
right in front of everyone.

RCO: During rush hour, even if you're on the train or bus well before it's set to go, stake a claim to a spot including a little extra personal space. Before you know it, things will fill up and that space will be violated if you don't grab a firm toehold.

RCO: "Does this train go to Newark?" Why would one passenger ask another that question? Unless they're going to Newark, or has memorized the train schedule, that passenger won't know. He/she will just know about their own stop.

RCO: With all their lurching, stopping, and going, I would bet that engineers are initially trained as New York taxi drivers.

PENN PANIC

RCO: Unofficial survey—out of the 9 million commuting through New York, 6.37 million of them lack sufficient common sense.

RCO: Be sure to always carry train or bus schedules for not only your station but any station that's anywhere remotely near your home. That way, if your regular method of conveyance is delayed or cancelled, you'll have a plan B, C, even D, to at least get close to home.

RCO: When you're walking through the hectic maze of the train or bus station, choose a blocker ahead of you, someone who seems like they are walking in the same direction as you. Then they can do all the blocking of oncoming pedestrian traffic and you can simply sneak in behind them.

RCO: Phantom bad breath is hard to handle on a crowded train or bus. You never know where it's coming from, so you don't know how to get away from it.

RCO: If the train lurches and you literally go flying, make sure you don't accidentally barely step on the toe of an angry man from the West Indies who will want to have a fist fight with you. Not that that's ever happened to me.

RCO: Don't you love when people walk one way while their heads are turned in another direction?

RCO: It often seems like the odds are against you when you're commuting— like it's 5,000 to one. 5,000 people seem like they're walking towards you, and you're the only one walking in the other direction.

RCO: You'll get through the crowds quickly if you act like a pilot fish, staying nearly adhered to the back of the shark winding his way through.

RCO: I could get rich selling tissues and cough drops on the train.

RCO: Less talk, more walk.

RACCOON RIDING SUBWAY ELICITS STRONG REACTIONS FROM NEW YORKERS

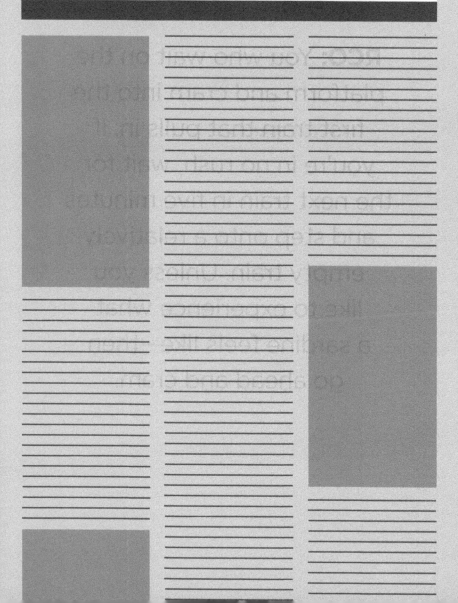

RCO: You who wait on the platform and cram into the first train that pulls in: if you're in no rush, wait for the next train in five minutes and step onto a relatively empty train. Unless you like to experience what a sardine feels like—then go ahead and cram.

RCO: With all the people I encounter on my commute, I wonder if some of them are there just for the free escalator rides.

RCO: I should bring a little card table on the train and sell deodorant. Better yet—I'll do everyone a favor and administer it myself to those who need it.

RCO: It would be smart of NJ Transit to monitor how many people get off at each station. Then maybe they can tailor the commute to the actual clientele. For example, if they just sent an hourly express train to the busiest stations, then there might be available seats on everyone else's train.

RCO: SBD* on the train today. Wasn't me. (*Silent But Deadly)

RCO: Every morning, it's an adventure once I arrive at Penn Station. You never know where the stairway you take up from the platform will lead you. Once in a while, I find myself standing on the street, not knowing how I got there. Other times, it's like one of those bad horror movies where doors and hallways lead to...a closed door!

RCO: Is it me, or does the train platform smell like a bus-station men's room? Maybe they buy their air freshener from the same supplier. Or not.

RCO: I really think there's something to The Force. When people stand too close to me, I often find myself saying almost audibly (or maybe they can hear me?!): "You don't want to stand here, you want to go to the next car." I even slightly wave my hand with a flourish, à la Obi-Wan Kenobi. And sometimes it works, and they move. Thanks, George Lucas!

RCO: I've come to the conclusion that there are a lot of schlumps in the world.

RCO: I find it terribly disconcerting, getting dripped on by a rogue air-conditioning unit while walking down the NYC sidewalk. At least I think/ hope it was water.

RCO: Ahh, Spring. Signs of new life. You see Mr. Robin on your lawn, tulips are popping up through the frosty ground, and Body Odor has returned to your commute.

RCO: Oh, who me?
No, I wasn't getting off at
the next step. But I thought
I would stand here, right
in the way, as 400 other
people try to get off.

RCO: I look around at my fellow commuters sometimes and realize I'm not in such bad shape after all.

RCO: Dig those pleather shorts. They look marvy on you, sir!

RCO: I saw someone try to go up a down escalator today. The same person twice.

RCO: When I see five cops in riot gear at the subway station, I don't know whether to feel secure or concerned.

RCO: When the train is this crowded, why can't you just find a spot and stay put?!

RCO: If I had a piece of the action and made a few shekels on everyone who played Candy Crush on their commutes, I'd be rich.

THE SUMMER OF AGONY MAY NEVER END

RCO: I consider walking on an escalator as getting exercise (as opposed to riding motionless).

RCO: While walking down the sidewalk today, I saw a woman spit in the street. Stay classy, New York!

Meet my commuting friends:
There's Huggy Bear, all
dressed in a seersucker suit,
brown penny loafers, straw
hat. He's probably the most
nattily dressed person on
the train. Reminds me of
Starsky & Hutch's buddy.

RCO: What if the crazy man I see every day, mumbling and yelling at anyone who passes him on the sidewalk is really saying something important? Maybe he's the enlightened one.

RCO: God has
a sense of humor.

RCO: Why am I always lucky enough to catch the guy picking his nose, just when I happen to look up from my newspaper?!

RCO: The other day, I spotted, for the first time ever, a New York City street sweeper. Not sure how effective he was since he was literally traveling about 50 mph up 8th Avenue.

(Credit: Public domain)

RCO: Walking under an umbrella along a rush-hour sidewalk, you have to act simultaneously like Gene Kelly in *Singing in the Rain*, while jousting like Sir Lancelot.

RCO: Dude, who you talking to?

RCO: The City is the only place at which you can give directions by smell. "To get to my office, you walk along 33rd, when you get to the rotten egg smell, turn onto 8th. Go three blocks, pass the garbage heap, and when you reach the smell of puke, turn left. Can't miss it!"

(Credit: Public domain)

RCO: Every day, I walk past a hotel that reads, "Introducing our new brand." Is the scaffolding that's been in front of that building for three years, with no other construction in sight, part of their "new brand"?

RCO: I never get bitten by a mosquito in New York. Have the rats eaten all the mosquitoes?

RCO: I need little more to get through my day than my reading glasses, train ticket, wallet, and a pen.

RCO: For about a week, there was a dirty puddle at the corner by my work, over a sewer grate. Instead of clearing the clog so the puddle could dissipate, NYC DPW decided it was better to just put cones around the puddle so no one would walk in it. Priceless.

(Credit: Public domain)

RCO: The painted crosswalks in The City are merely just suggestions, apparently. Everyone jaywalks—even cops— and no one seems to be concerned that they are holding up traffic.

MICHAEL LEWIS

RCO: Surface temperature
on Mars = summer on a
Penn Station train platform

RCO: Sometimes I suppose it can be a little confusing to figure out how to open the door between the train car. But instead of just helping the person, let's all just watch them struggle.

Meet my commuting friends:
There's the Quiet Car Nazi.
Don't say a word
(not even one), because
if you do, you'll wake
him, he'll pop up his head
from the seat like a prairie
dog, and he will angrily
remind you not to talk.

RCO: I'm such a creature of habit, walking in my own footsteps day after day. If an escalator I always take happens to be running in the wrong direction for some reason, I usually step onto it anyway before I realize what's happening.

SUMMER OF HELL

RCO: Sometimes when you're walking along the sidewalk, a hottie in front of you is like a carrot on a stick, leading you forward.

RCO: You'd think that if you found a spot and stood still that people wouldn't walk into you. Think not.

RCO: Commuter survival of the fittest—locate the old, slow, distracted person and pass them to be the last person on the train.

RCO: To commute in style between train cars, bring your own stool (that stows nicely into your backpack).

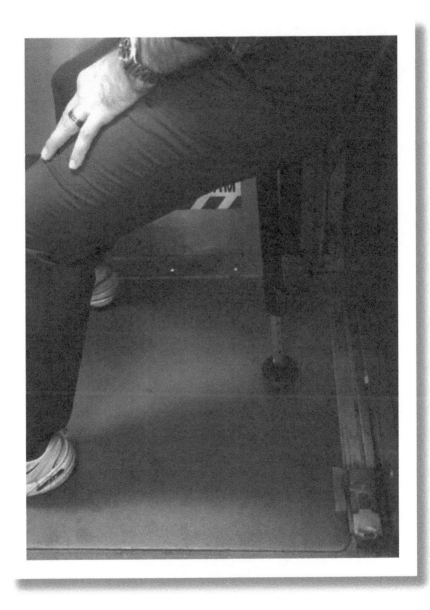

RCO: Subway or NY Penn—
same stench, different pile.

RCO: Crosswalk timers can be helpful to drivers, so you know whether to speed up or slow down. (Thanks, Rachel Montgomery.)

RCO: I keep seeing people eating popcorn on the train ride home. I wonder where they're getting this delicacy.

RCO: I know I'm bone-tired at the end of the day when I screw up even the one-star Sudoku puzzles.

RCO: Sometimes in the morning, I feel like I'm sleepwalking with my eyes open.

RCO: I can tolerate your banging into me once. But twice? Really?

RCO: I feel so old-school—people are playing on their cellphones and I'm here with my newspaper Sudoku puzzle and pen.

RCO: Sometimes the train ride seems like a reckless, careening Nantucket sleigh ride. Other times, it can't get out of its own way.

RCO: Not enough people brush their teeth.

RCO: Look out the window as you approach Penn Station. It will prepare you to locate the nearest exit stair, either left or right, and will better prepare you to quickly exit.

RCO: A chiropractor should set up a table on the train platform and give adjustments.

RCO: Not sure why soldiers protecting us in Penn Station wear camouflage. Perhaps the traditional camouflage pattern should be replaced with designs of skyscrapers and graffiti. (But I appreciate the soldiers being there!)

RCO: There was a fatality on our train line? I suppose it sounds cold but—please finish the investigation quickly so service can resume and the rest of us can get where we need to go.

RCO: A morbidly obese person sat on me on the train today. Good times.

RIDERS FACE ANOTHER MESSY COMMUTE

RCO: Sometimes my fellow commuter's iPod is so loud I can almost play Name That Tune.

RCO: It's so hot in Penn Station sometimes that just walking outside into the summer heat seems like air conditioning.

RCO: Nice to come home part of the year and have it still be light outside.

Meet my commuting friends:
Oh, great, I'm sitting
near Mr. Hairball, the guy
who clears his throat
every twelve seconds.

RCO: You would think that standing on the platform in one place for twenty minutes would stop people from walking into you. But no, here comes a guy, not looking up from his phone. I had to whistle or he would have run right into me.

RCO: When the sun's out, I try to grab some vitamin D at lunchtime.

RCO: The train makes such a wide-banked turn between the transfer station and the tunnel under the Hudson that it feels as if we all need to lean the other way, or the train might roll over.

RCO: When it rains, half the people in NYC use an umbrella. The other half aren't happy about it, and might even slap your umbrella out of your hand.

TRAIN DERAILS EN ROUTE TO PENN STATION

RCO: Sorry that you have all of that luggage to tote around through one of the world's busiest train stations, but do you really have to just drop those bags at the top of the stairs so no one else can pass?

RCO: What's up with you? You can't look away from your smartphone long enough to watch where you're going?

RCO: The tunnel, just outside of Penn Station, seems like a giant cave, but one with trains, tracks, 100-degree heat and humidity, and no stalactites. You know, come to think of it, it doesn't seem like a cave at all.

FIRST DAYS WILL BE TOUGH ON COMMUTERS

RCO: People have the worst B.O. at the end of the day. Time to travel with Vicks VapoRub to swab under my nose.

RCO: Am I fanning myself because it's hot? No, I'm fanning the sweat-stink back at the perpetrator.

RCO: Every first snowfall should be declared a national holiday, called Everyone Forgets How to Drive Day. (Thanks, Rachel Montgomery.)

RCO: I never noticed before, but all sweat kinda smells the same. Regardless of the sweat-or.

RCO: Is there anywhere I can buy little personal-size spray bottles of Febreze?

RCO: I never had an escalator stop mid-ride. Until today.

RCO: I swear my right arm is getting longer than my left, as I carry this heavy bag back and forth every day.

RCO: When squished like a sardine, don't move.

RCO: They need more benches on the train platform.

MICHAEL LEWIS

RCO: Are your legs painted on?

RCO: The nearest exit may be behind you – don't just line up behind someone standing at the train door (and then get stuck waiting while they leisurely saunter off the train, and make you miss your stop). There may be no one waiting at the other train door that's behind you. (Thanks Eric Brandon)

RCO: It's discouraging, with your first steps into Penn Station, to be hit with the wafted scent of sweat.

RCO: Do those who get mad at people on the Quiet Car work on the firing range? (Thanks, Joe Potestivo.)

RCO: Sometimes on the platform, you feel like you're on the Titanic and the last lifeboat has left.

(Credit: Public Domain)

RCO: Hold onto your hairpiece; sometimes it's like a wind tunnel on the platform.

RCO: Strange how in NYC the temperature can vary ten degrees from one street to the next.

RCO: I walk fast not because I'm in a rush, but because I want to get away from slow people.

RCO: Sometimes you've got to weave through the train station like a chainsaw through an ice sculpture.

Meet my commuting friends:
There's Friar ____
(Use your imagination;
rhymes with...). I named
him for his unique hairdo—
perfect bald circle on top,
ring of hair around his head.

RCO: Walking the sidewalks
of New York, it may seem
like you've arrived at
the Tower of Babel.

RIDERSHIP SWELLS AS COMMUTERS LOOK FOR RELIEF

RCO: After you.
Ladies first.
But if you're focused
on your phone and not
paying attention—no.

RCO: I would love it if the makers of Raid, Cold-EEZE, and Lysol got together to invent a "personal yard guard" that each of us commuters could spray on ourselves to thwart the germs and bad breath spewed at us by thoughtless/carefree commuters who are probably too sick to be going to work, but they thought they'd cough, sneeze, and clear their throats on us anyway.

RCO: Once the train starts moving, they should prohibit people from moving car to car. Stay put, people!

RCO: I'm thinking ahead and bracing for impact. This guy's not holding on and he's about to fall on me.

RCO: Never fails—
one of those long articulated
buses always seems to block
the crosswalk right as the
light is about to change,
so no one can walk.

RCO: How can someone have B.O. that bad and it's not even 7:30AM yet?!

RCO: Seeing a dad holding his toddler daughter on the train, I get choked up. Where has the time gone?

RCO: That's a first—a guy using dip on his commute, and spitting into a coffee cup. That's gross no matter what the location.

RCO: Are sweaty people aware that they smell? Does a skunk smell himself?

RCO: Do rules of the Quiet Car also apply to those who talk to themselves? Or think loudly?

RCO: I feel like I'm running an obstacle course, and the obstacles are moving too.

RCO: I wear earplugs on the train as much to tune out the people as to muffle the noise when I stand between cars.

RCO: If we look down the track, all at the same time, all awaiting the arrival of the late train, maybe by the sheer power of our collective angst, we can will the train to arrive.

RCO: It's as if I'm canoeing, trying to find the channel that runs through the rocks of the train station, so I can quickly run through.

RCO: Attention, train-station announcers—Can you learn how to pronounce station stops? The train goes to Suffern, not "sufferin'."

REPAIRS FAR FROM FINISHED

RCO: As part of their training, engineers should be made to ride between train cars and see what it's like to try to stand as someone stomps on the brake and gas pedals.

RCO: Kinda sux when a train going to the same destination arrives on the adjacent track but everyone's already crammed onto your train.

RCO: Running ahead of me rudely onto the train, you'd better be pregnant or bleeding.

RCO: The train can't leave until I get on it.

(Credit: Public domain)

RCO: Don't let their pleasant little twinkling bell fool you; the bikes barreling along the bike path on 8th Ave will always catch you unawares and lay you out.

RCO: It's a special kind of disturbing when a total stranger falls asleep on you, on the bus or train— especially when you've got to get off the next stop.

RCO: When choosing which train car to board, there is a completely foolproof way to identify which one has no empty seats. It's always the one you decided to enter. (Thanks, Steven Schragis).

RCO: Good morning, sir.
I guess what's in your bag
must be very important,
more important than
the people standing
in the aisle who would
appreciate the seat that
your bag is enjoying.
(Thanks, Gail Burke.)

RCO: Meet my commuting friends: There's poopy boy. I wish I had a nickel for every time he uses the bathroom on the train. Kinda feel sorry for him.

RCO: Don't settle for the local bus when you wanted the express. It would be quicker to walk.

RCO: People line up like lemmings, crowded together to go through the open door. Why doesn't anyone make the Herculean effort to open the closed door right next to it so twice as many people can go through? (Thanks, Joe Potestivo.)

RCO: My morning commute finds me and millions of other people rushing to get to a place we really don't want to be.

(Credit: Public domain)

RCO: If they continue to operate antique trains, I'm thinking we should pay our fare in wampum, fur pelts, and magic beans.

RCO: Anyone wonder why the slowest commute time of the day is called Rush Hour?

COMMUTERS BRACING FOR A ROUGH RIDE

RCO: I spend more hours in my day with strangers on the train than I do with my own loving family.

RCO: Sometimes you need a shoehorn to step into the train.

RCO: Always carry hand sanitizer with you. Always.

RCO: The train is a little like church, where everyone sits in the same seat every time and woe to the person who dares to sit in someone's "assigned" pew—I mean, seat. (Thanks, Chris Anderson.)

RCO: I used to think things
and hold my tongue.
Not no more. #nofilter

RCO: Not sure what I dislike more—mass-transit announcers that sound like Charlie Brown's teacher or computer voices that creep me out and mispronounce every other word.

RCO: Have a nice trip.
See you next fall.

RCO: Sometimes you excitedly step into an empty train car and soon discover why it's empty. For example—no A/C on the hottest day of the summer, or the homeless dude is sprawled across the seats and his odor permeates your entire being. (Thanks, Bob Jenny.)

IT COULD BE WORSE

RCO: No matter how bad your commute, it still beats driving.

(Credit: Rgoogin at the English language Wikipedia.)

AFTERWORD

Congratulations! You made it home from another day of hard work. You braved your unpleasant commute. Take a load off, melt into the couch for a few, grab a cold one, decompress, and enjoy your evening. I hope my Random Commuter Observations provided you with a smile, a chuckle, advice, or a sneer, or otherwise helped you in some way get through your trip.

I welcome your own RCOs—maybe they'll wind up in a future book! Send me your comments and input at SamsPop1@aol.com.

And just think – tomorrow you get to commute all over again. Happy travels!

ABOUT THE AUTHOR

Michael Lewis is the author/coauthor of eleven books, including *The 100 Best Beatles Songs*, *Outdated Advertising*, and *A Guy Walks Into a Bar*. A career communications professional, book editor, and chronic/cranky commuter, he has worked in publishing for more than 25 years. He lives in northern New Jersey and is looking for a new job with an easy commute.

ABOUT THE ILLUSTRATOR

Martha Washington is the nom de plume of
a longtime illustrator.